M000273031

Evidence-Based Inquiry Using Primary Sources

Grade 3

Credits
Author: Shirley Pearson
Copy Editor: Sandra Ogle

Visit *carsondellosa.com* for correlations to Common Core, state, national, and Canadian provincial standards.

Carson-Dellosa Publishing, LLC
PO Box 35665
Greensboro, NC 27425 USA
carsondellosa.com

ISBN 978-1-4838-2398-0
01-106157784

Table of Contents

Introduction 2

Performance Rubric 3

How to Use This Book. 3

Noteworthy Events

How Much Are *You* Worth? 4

After the War 8

My Voice Will Be Heard 12

Diverse Identities, Customs, and Traditions

Welcome to America! 16

Saving History. 20

An Education Dream . . . . . . : . . 24

Movement of Goods and People

Hit the Road! 28

Riding the Rails 32

The Worker as a Machine 36

American Heroes

A Complex Man 40

Passenger to Freedom 44

A Man of Many Words. 48

Natural Resources: Helping People Survive

Home Sweet Home 52

Gold Fever 56

Beneath the Ice 60

Answer Key 64

Introduction

The primary sources shown in this book represent glimpses of real life. They are photographs of actual people, posters that once hung on storefronts, paintings that interpret history, and ads or articles taken from newspapers in circulation in another era. All primary sources shown here are from the archives of the Library of Congress.

This book includes 15 primary sources. Each is accompanied by the same story written at three levels (below grade level, on grade level, and above grade level) for differentiation. Distribute the versions according to students' abilities. The final page of each selection offers prompts and questions about the primary source and/or text and can be used for all levels with some assistance.

This book is full of opportunities for inquiry-based learning. Inquiry-based learning is a process of active learning that greatly improves reading comprehension skills. Allow the primary sources reproduced on these pages to speak for themselves. Then, allow the natural curiosity of students to do the rest.

The role of the teacher in inquiry-based learning is that of facilitator. Teachers are encouraged to first present the primary source without much accompanying information. Encourage students to ask questions, look for answers, and form relationships between the past and the present. Prompt students to think critically about what they are viewing. Let them make inferences from the details, share varying points of view, draw conclusions, and connect known facts with picture details.

Performance Rubric

Use this rubric as a guide for assessing students' engagement with each primary source unit.

4	_____ Notes details and evaluates primary source critically
	_____ Displays avid curiosity and engagement with topic
	_____ Makes or disproves connections between primary source and his/her own experiences
	_____ Identifies research questions and finds answers
	_____ Exhibits high-level thinking skills when responding to _Investigate_, _Question_, and _Understand_ prompts
3	_____ Notes details and evaluates primary source superficially
	_____ Displays average curiosity about and engagement with topic
	_____ Makes obvious connections between primary source and his/her own experiences
	_____ Identifies research questions and finds answers with adult help
	_____ Responds adequately to _Investigate_, _Question_, and _Understand_ prompts
2	_____ Notes some details but cannot evaluate primary source
	_____ Displays some curiosity about and engagement with topic
	_____ Cannot see beyond obvious connections between primary source and his/her own experiences
	_____ Identifies research questions but is unable to find answers
	_____ Responds without insight or high-level thinking to _Investigate_, _Question_, and _Understand_ prompts
1	_____ Notes few details and does not evaluate primary source
	_____ Displays relative indifference toward topic
	_____ Is unable to see connections between primary source and his/her own experiences
	_____ Cannot identify research questions and does not follow up
	_____ Shows little interest in or is unable to respond thoughtfully to _Investigate_, _Question_, and _Understand_ prompts

How to Use This Book

Teachers may wish to prompt students to study each primary source before reading the accompanying text. Students can write or ask questions as they study the documents or photographs. Spark their curiosity with discussion about the elements of the primary source. Students may then discover more information in the text. An inquiry page follows each set of texts and provides three levels of prompts: _Investigate_, _Question_, and _Understand_. Allow time and opportunity for students to answer their own questions and to find out more in books, magazines, and on safe Internet sources.

How Much Are *You* Worth?

This 1835 poster was printed by Thomas Griggs. He was a slave trader in Charleston, South Carolina. Posters like this were common before the Civil War.

Slavery had come to America years earlier. Half a million African slaves were sent to the colonies. This trade ended in 1808. But, American slavery didn't end. Slaves didn't have rights like white people did. Slaves were owned. If a woman was a slave, her children were too. More American slaves were born.

Most northern farms were small. Farmers did all the work themselves. Many southern farms were big. Southern farmers grew crops like cotton. Cotton made a lot of money. Farmers needed many people to work in the cotton fields. Who were these workers? American slaves.

Slave trading was a big business. Slave traders bought slaves. The slaves were held in jails called "slave pens." Later, they were shipped south. There, slave traders sold slaves for high prices. In 1836 alone, more than 100,000 slaves were traded from Virginia to the Deep South.

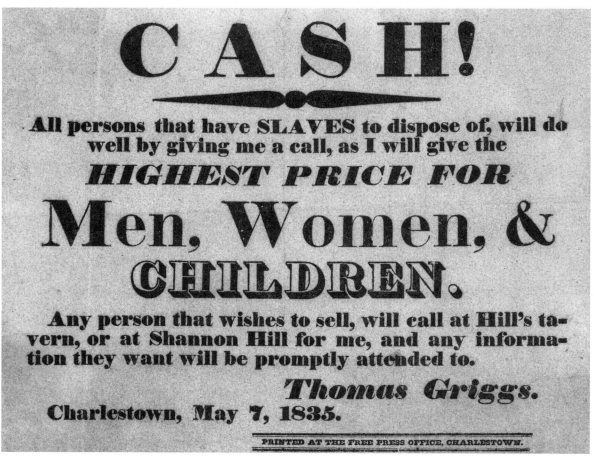

CASH!

All persons that have SLAVES to dispose of, will do well by giving me a call, as I will give the

HIGHEST PRICE FOR

Men, Women, &

CHILDREN.

Any person that wishes to sell, will call at Hill's tavern, or at Shannon Hill for me, and any information they want will be promptly attended to.

Thomas Griggs.

Charlestown, May 7, 1835.

PRINTED AT THE FREE PRESS OFFICE, CHARLESTOWN.

Library of Congress, LC-USZ62-62799

How Much Are *You* Worth?

This 1835 poster was printed by Thomas Griggs, a slave trader in Charleston, South Carolina. Such posters were common before the Civil War.

Slavery had come to America centuries earlier. The transatlantic slave trade brought half a million slaves to the colonies. In 1808, the African slave trade ended. But, this didn't stop the slave trade in America. Slaves didn't have rights like white people did. Slaves were owned. If slaveholders owned women, they owned the women's children too. The American-born slave population increased.

Most northern farms were small. Farmers didn't need outside help. Many southern farms, called plantations, were big. Cotton plantations made a lot of money. They needed many people to work in the fields. Who were these workers? American slaves.

Slave trading was a profitable business. Slave traders bought slaves. Slaves were held in jails called "slave pens." Then, the slaves were shipped to the southern states, where they were sold for a higher price. In 1836 alone, over 100,000 slaves were traded from Virginia to the Deep South.

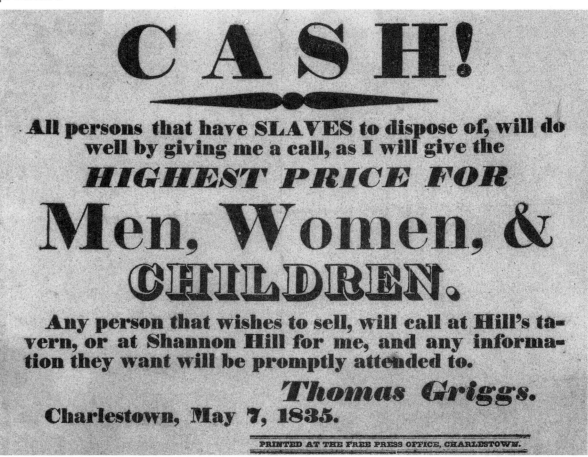

Library of Congress, LC-USZ62-62799

How Much Are *You* Worth?

Posters like this 1835 advertisement, or broadside, printed by Charleston, South Carolina, slave trader Thomas Griggs, were common before the Civil War.

Slavery had come to America centuries earlier. The transatlantic slave trade sent half a million slaves to the colonies. In 1808, the African slave trade ended. But, this didn't end slavery or the slave trade in America. Slaves didn't have rights, like white people; slaves were considered property. If an enslaved woman had children, her slaveholder owned her children too. The American-born slave population increased.

Northern farmers ran their small farms themselves. Many southern farmers had big plantations. Cotton plantations were very profitable and required many people to work in the fields. Where did these workers come from? The American slave trade.

Slave trading was a moneymaking business. Slave traders bought slaves and held them in jails, called "slave pens." Then, the slaves were shipped to southern states where they were sold for a profit. In 1836 alone, over 100,000 slaves were traded from Virginia to the Deep South.

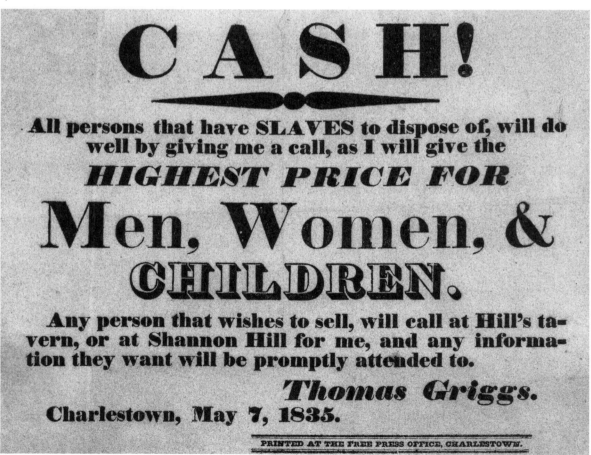

Library of Congress, LC-USZ62-62799

 © Carson-Dellosa • CD-104861 • Evidence-Based Inquiry Using Primary Sources

Name _____

How Much Are *You* Worth?

 Investigate

1. Think of a sign in a newspaper or store window that you may have seen recently. Does this poster remind you of that sign? Why or why not?

_____

_____

2. Look closely at the poster. What clues tell you that slavery was a business? Explain.

_____

_____

? Question

3. Is slavery *legal* in any country today? Does slavery still exist? If you don't know, look in books and on safe Internet sites to find out.

_____

_____

4. Do you think Mr. Griggs paid the same amount for every slave he bought? What sort of slave do you think would cost him more money? Less money? Why?

_____

_____

Understand

5. Imagine being a slave bought by Mr. Griggs. Describe what might happen to you.

_____

_____

6. Give two reasons why slaveholders might want to sell their slave(s). Write your answers in complete sentences.

_____

_____

After the War

By 1861, the United States included 34 states. Some states had slaves. Other states didn't want slavery. Some southern slave states chose to leave the Union. They became the Confederate States of America. Confederate troops attacked Union troops at Fort Sumter in Charleston, South Carolina. This began the Civil War.

Confederate troops moved north. Union troops moved south. They traveled by foot, horseback, or train. Troops on the coast used ships. Whenever they met, they fought. No one wanted the enemy to be able to fight again. They destroyed bridges and railroads. They burned food storage buildings. Wounded soldiers didn't get proper care. People didn't get enough to eat.

The Confederates stopped fighting in 1865. This ended the war. This ended slavery too. Close to 700,000 people had died. Nearly four million slaves were free.

Photography was new. Photographs could show people what war had done. This photograph was taken by George Barnard. The war had just ended. Barnard was a war photographer. This photograph shows Charleston, South Carolina, in 1865. This was where the war had started.

Library of Congress, LC-B8171-3448

After the War

By 1861, the nation included 34 states. Some states, mostly southern, allowed slavery. Others, mostly northern, didn't want slavery spreading into new states. Some slave states decided to leave the Union, creating the Confederate States of America. Confederate troops attacked Union troops at Fort Sumter in Charleston, South Carolina, starting the Civil War.

Confederate armies moved north. Union armies moved south. Troops near the coast used ships, but most travel was on foot, horseback, or train. The generals didn't just want to win battles. They wanted to ensure the enemy couldn't fight again. They destroyed bridges and railroads. They burned food storage buildings. Wounded soldiers didn't receive proper care. Food was scarce.

The Confederacy surrendered in 1865. Close to 700,000 people had died. The war ended; so did slavery. Nearly four million slaves were free.

Photography was still a new invention. Photographs could show people what war had done. This photograph was taken by war photographer George Barnard in 1865. The war had just ended. This photograph shows Charleston, South Carolina, the place where the war had begun.

After the War

By 1861, the nation included 34 states. Some states, mostly southern, allowed slavery. Others, mostly northern, didn't want slavery moving into new states. Eleven slave states left the Union to form the Confederate States of America. Confederate troops attacked Union troops at Fort Sumter in Charleston, South Carolina, starting the Civil War.

Confederate forces moved north. Union forces moved south. Troops along the coast were able to travel by ship, but most movement was on foot, horseback, or train. The generals didn't only want to win; they wanted to ensure the enemy couldn't fight again. They destroyed bridges and railroads. They burned food storage buildings, causing food shortages. Wounded soldiers were unable to receive proper care.

The Confederacy surrendered in 1865. Almost 700,000 people had died, but, thanks to the 13th Amendment, nearly four million slaves were free.

Photography was relatively new. Photographs could show people the effects of war. This photo was taken by war photographer George Barnard in 1865 after the war had ended. It shows Charleston, the place where the war had begun.

Library of Congress, LC-B8171-3448

Name _____

After the War

 Investigate

1. What did you notice first about the photo? Why?

    _____

    _____

2. Examine the buildings in the photograph. Describe the differences you see.

    _____

    _____

 Question

3. How do you think people living in destroyed cities survived after the war? Read more about Reconstruction after the Civil War in books or on safe Internet sites.

    _____

    _____

4. After studying this photograph, what do you want to learn more about?

    _____

    _____

 Understand

5. Based on this text and the photograph, do you think the Civil War needed to have been fought? Why or why not?

    _____

    _____

6. Imagine you are one of the people in this photograph in 1865. Describe your emotions.

    _____

    _____

My Voice Will Be Heard

Are you American? Are you 18? Then, you can vote. It doesn't matter what you look like. It doesn't matter what you have. It doesn't matter what you do. You still have the right to vote.

Who voted for George Washington? Not many people could vote in 1789. Voters were men. They were 21. They were white. They were Protestant Christians. And, they owned property.

Laws changed. The Civil War started in 1865. Almost all white adult males could vote. Then, slavery ended. Laws changed again. Women could vote in 1920. Eighteen-year-olds could vote in 1971.

This print was created by Alfred Waud. It is titled "The First Vote." It appeared on a *Harper's Weekly* cover in November 1867. The 15th Amendment was passed in 1870. This law gave African American men the right to vote. But, later laws made voting difficult for African Americans. Another civil rights movement took place in the 1960s. In 1965, President Lyndon Johnson passed the Voting Rights Act. This finally gave African Americans, and poor Americans, the real freedom to vote.

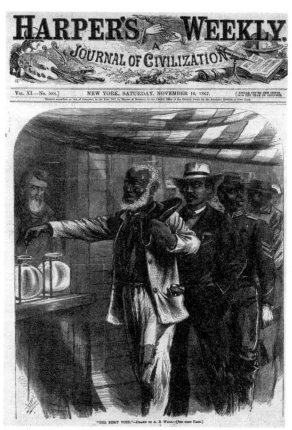

Library of Congress, LC-USZ62-19234

My Voice Will Be Heard

If you're an 18-year-old American, you can vote. Regardless of what you look like, what you have, or what you do—you still have the right to vote.

Who elected George Washington? In 1789, few people could vote. These voters were men. They were 21. They were white. They were Protestant Christians. And, they owned property. Most people couldn't vote.

Laws changed as circumstances changed. By the time the Civil War started, almost all white adult males were eligible to vote. Slavery ended. Laws changed again. By 1920, women could vote. By 1971, 18-year-olds could vote.

This print, "The First Vote," was created by Alfred Waud. It appeared on the cover of *Harper's Weekly* in November 1867 several years before the 15th Amendment was passed in 1870. This law gave African American men the right to vote. But, later laws made voting difficult for African Americans. In 1965, President Lyndon Johnson passed the Voting Rights Act. It took this second civil rights movement before African Americans—and poor Americans—were truly free to vote.

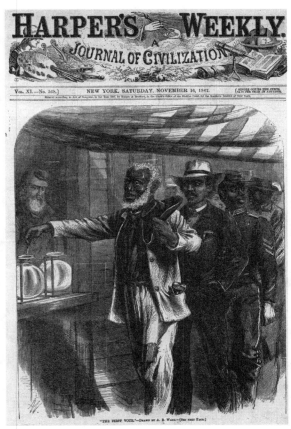

Library of Congress, LC-USZ62-19234

My Voice Will Be Heard

If you're an 18-year-old American, you're eligible to vote. Regardless of your appearance, your possessions, or your employment—you still have the right to vote.

Who elected George Washington? In 1789, eligible voters were white males over 21 who were Protestant Christians and owned property. This meant that the majority of Americans couldn't vote.

Laws changed as circumstances changed. At the time of the Civil War, almost all white adult males were eligible to vote. After the war, laws changed again. Slavery was abolished. By 1920, women could vote; by 1971, 18-year-olds were eligible as well.

This print, titled "The First Vote," was created by Alfred Waud. It appeared on the November 1867 cover of *Harper's Weekly* several years before the 15th Amendment was passed in 1870. This amendment gave black men the right to vote. But, later laws made voting difficult for African Americans. In 1965, President Lyndon Johnson passed the Voting Rights Act. It took this second civil rights movement of the 1960s before African Americans—and poor Americans—were truly free to vote.

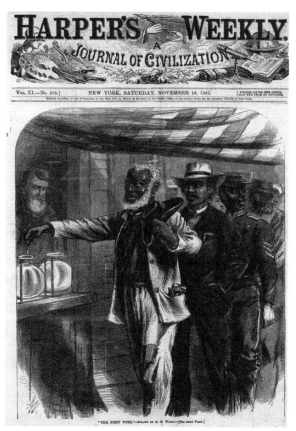

Library of Congress, LC-USZ62-19234

Name _____

My Voice Will Be Heard

 Investigate

1. What is happening in this print?

   _____

   _____

2. Look at the men's clothing. What do you think these men do for a living?

   _____

   _____

Question

3. Study the men in this print. Describe some differences between the man on the left and the four men on the right. What do you think the artist is trying to tell the reader?

   _____

   _____

4. Why do you think this print was published before the 15th Amendment became law?

   _____

   _____

Understand

5. Do you think everyone should have the right to vote? Do you think certain people should not be allowed to vote? Explain your answer.

   _____

   _____

6. What things are so important to you that you would want to be able to vote on them?

   _____

   _____

Welcome to America!

The Pilgrims were some of America's first immigrants. Different people have flocked to the United States at different times. The first settlers created the colonies. Later immigrants farmed the Midwest. After the Civil War, immigration boomed. Millions of Eastern Europeans fled their homes. They headed to America. They worked in factories. Philadelphia and New York City exploded in size.

By 1910, New York City was full of immigrants. Three-quarters of New Yorkers were born elsewhere, or their parents had been. Thousands of Jews lived in the city's Lower East Side. They spoke Yiddish. They kept their Jewish faith. Many Jewish men were peddlers. Many Jewish women and children worked in unsafe clothing factories. Some brought their work home. Homes were small and crowded.

The Jewish calendar starts in the fall. This 1911 photograph was taken on New York City's East Side. It shows a boy during the Jewish New Year. He's wearing a prayer shawl with fringes. Many Jews celebrate the New Year with sweets. Apples dipped in honey are common treats. They symbolize the hope for a "sweet" new year.

Library of Congress, LC-USZ62-38119

Welcome to America!

The Pilgrims were some of America's first immigrants. Different people have flocked to the United States at different times. The first settlers created the colonies. Later, immigrants farmed the Midwest. After the Civil War, immigration boomed. Millions of Eastern Europeans fled poverty and suffering. They headed to cities where factories provided work. Philadelphia and New York City exploded in size.

By 1910, three-quarters of New Yorkers were born in a foreign country, or their parents had been. The world's greatest number of Jews lived in the city's Lower East Side. They spoke Yiddish and practiced their Jewish faith. Clothing was a huge industry. Most Jewish women and children worked in clothing factories. Some worked at home in small and crowded rooms. Many Jewish men were peddlers.

The Jewish calendar begins in the fall. This 1911 photograph was taken on New York City's East Side. It shows a boy wearing a prayer shawl with fringes during the Jewish New Year. Many Jews celebrate the New Year with sweets. Apples dipped in honey are common treats. They symbolize the hope for a "sweet" new year.

Library of Congress, LC-USZ62-38119

Welcome to America!

The Pilgrims were some of America's first immigrants. Different people have flocked to the country at different times. The first settlers formed the colonies. Later, immigrants moved into the Midwest. People settled together to preserve their language and customs. After the Civil War, immigration boomed. Millions of Eastern Europeans fled poverty and persecution. Cities like Philadelphia and New York City exploded in size.

By 1910, three-quarters of New Yorkers or their parents were born in a foreign country. The greatest number of Jews in the world lived in the city's Lower East Side. They brought with them their Yiddish language and Jewish faith. Most Jewish women and children worked in the garment industry, either in factories or at home. Many Jewish men were peddlers.

The Jewish calendar begins in September or October. This photograph was taken on New York City's East Side during the 1911 Jewish New Year. The boy is wearing a prayer shawl with fringes. Many Jews celebrate the New Year by eating sweets. Apples dipped in honey are common treats that symbolize the hope for a "sweet" new year.

Library of Congress, LC-USZ62-38119

Welcome to America!

 Investigate

1. What photographic clues tell you this is a special day?

    _____

    _____

2. Looking only at the photo, do you think this photograph was taken in an area with many Jewish residents? Explain your answer.

    _____

    _____

? **Question**

3. Based on the text, why do you think so many immigrants settled in large cities?

    _____

    _____

4. Can anyone who wants to move to the United States? What are the rules? If you don't know, look in books and on safe Internet sites to find out.

    _____

    _____

 Understand

5. How do you think this boy might have spent his time on a day when it was not a special holiday? Answer using complete sentences.

    _____

    _____

6. Imagine you were an immigrant in 1911. Where would you want your family to live? Why?

    _____

    _____

Saving History

The word *Hopi* means "peaceful people." The Hopi are one of the oldest American Indian tribes. The nation's oldest town is the Hopi village of Old Oraibi. The Hopi Reservation is in northeastern Arizona.

The Hopi are a Pueblo people. Women are important. Women give land to their daughters. Men live in their wives' homes. The Hopi used to be hunters and gatherers. When they settled in Arizona, they became farmers. They made the high, flat mesas their home. Their multifamily stone houses were called pueblos. Arizona has a desert climate. But, the Hopi were still able to grow crops. They grew corn, squash, and beans. Corn is sacred to the Hopi. Cornmeal is used in many ceremonies.

Photographer Edward S. Curtis took this photo in 1906. American Indians were being forced onto reservations. Curtis staged many of his photos to show specific traditions. This photograph shows Hopi women grinding corn. Unmarried girls wore their hair in twists. They wound their hair around corn husks or pieces of wood. Then, they removed the wood. These twists are called squash-blossom whorls.

Library of Congress, LC-USZ62-94089

Saving History

Hopi means "peaceful people." Many American Indian tribes exist. The Hopi were one of the first. The nation's oldest town is the Hopi village of Old Oraibi. The Hopi Reservation is in northeastern Arizona.

The Hopi are a Pueblo people. Women are important. Daughters inherit land from their mothers. Men live with their wives' families. The Hopi used to be hunters and gatherers. By the time they settled in Arizona, they were farmers. They built multifamily stone houses, called pueblos, on the high mesas. Despite the desert climate, the Hopi grew crops. They harvested corn, squash, and beans. Corn is sacred to the Hopi. Cornmeal is often used as an offering during rituals.

Photographer Edward S. Curtis lived at a time when American Indians were being forced onto reservations. Curtis wanted to record their way of life, so he staged many of his photos to demonstrate Hopi traditions. This 1906 photograph shows Hopi women grinding corn. Unmarried girls twisted their hair around corn husks or pieces of wood and then removed the wood. The twists are called squash-blossom whorls.

Saving History

Hopi means "peaceful people." The Hopi are one of the oldest American Indian tribes. The nation's earliest town is the Hopi village of Old Oraibi. The Hopi Reservation is located in northeastern Arizona.

The Hopi are a Pueblo people. They are a matrilineal society. This means that ancestry and property passes from mother to daughter. Originally, the Hopi were hunters and gatherers. By the time they settled in Arizona, the Hopi had become farmers. They built their multifamily stone houses, called pueblos, on high mesas. Even in the desert climate, the Hopi were able to grow crops such as corn, squash, and beans. Corn is sacred to the Hopi. Cornmeal is often used as an offering during rituals.

Photographer Edward S. Curtis lived at a time when American Indians were being forced onto reservations. Curtis wanted to record their vanishing way of life. He staged many of his photos to preserve specific traditions. This 1906 photograph shows young Hopi women grinding corn. Unmarried girls twisted their hair around corn husks or pieces of wood and then removed the wood, creating squash-blossom whorls.

Library of Congress, LC-USZ62-94089

Name _____

Saving History

 Investigate

1. What did you notice first about this photograph? Why?

   _____

   _____

2. Describe some of the tools you see. Use complete sentences.

   _____

   _____

? Question

3. What do you wonder about these women?

   _____

   _____

4. Do you think this is a natural photograph or a planned photograph? Why?

   _____

   _____

Understand

5. Imagine living in a Hopi pueblo in 1906. How would your life be different?

   _____

   _____

6. Study the entire photograph. Read more about Hopi traditions in books or on safe Internet sites to discover the importance of what these women are doing. Write about what you have found out.

   _____

   _____

An Education Dream

Education is important. Soon after the Pilgrims arrived, laws stated that towns must have schools. Attending school wasn't always easy. Before the Civil War, few African Americans went to school. It was illegal in many states.

In 1870, four in five freed slaves couldn't read or write. Schools were built across the South. Little money went to "colored" schools, as they were called. But, African Americans still came. By 1900, one in three black children attended school.

Booker T. Washington was born a slave. He became an Alabama teacher. In 1881, he started the Tuskegee Normal School for Colored Teachers. Students learned practical skills. Washington hoped they would become teachers. He had to raise money for his school. Photojournalists like Frances Benjamin Johnston helped. Her photographs persuaded rich people to donate funds.

Johnston took this photograph in 1902. It shows the one-room Annie Davis School. The students are studying corn and cotton. This school was part of the Tuskegee Institute. Tuskegee Institute schools were much better supplied than other African American schools at the time.

Library of Congress, LC-USZ62-78481

An Education Dream

Education is important to Americans. Soon after the Pilgrims arrived, laws stated that towns must have schools. Attending school wasn't always easy. Before the Civil War, few African Americans went to school. It was illegal in many states.

In 1870, four in five freed slaves couldn't read or write. Schools were built across the South. Little money went to "colored" schools, as they were called, but African Americans still wanted an education. By 1900, one in three black children attended school.

A former slave named Booker T. Washington started Alabama's Tuskegee Normal School for Colored Teachers in 1881. Washington wanted students to learn practical skills. He hoped they would become teachers. Washington needed to raise money for his school. Photojournalists like Frances Benjamin Johnston helped. Her photographs persuaded rich people to donate funds.

Johnston took this photograph of the one-room Annie Davis School in 1902. The students are studying corn and cotton. This school was part of the Tuskegee Institute. Schools like Annie Davis were much better supplied than other African American schools at the time.

Library of Congress, LC-USZ62-78481

An Education Dream

Education is important to Americans. Soon after the Pilgrims arrived, laws stated that towns must have schools. Going to school wasn't always easy, especially before the Civil War. It was illegal in many states for African Americans to be educated.

In 1870, four in five freed slaves couldn't read or write. Schools were built across the South. Little money went to "colored" schools, as they were called, but African Americans still wanted an education. By 1900, one in three black children attended school.

A former slave named Booker T. Washington started Alabama's Tuskegee Normal School for Colored Teachers in 1881. Washington wanted students to learn practical skills and become teachers. He needed to raise money for his school. Photojournalists like Frances Benjamin Johnston helped. Her photos persuaded rich people to donate funds.

Johnston took this photograph of the one-room Annie Davis School in 1902. The students are studying corn and cotton. This school was part of the Tuskegee Institute. Schools like Annie Davis were much better supplied than other African American schools at the time.

Library of Congress, LC-USZ62-78481

An Education Dream

🔍 Investigate

1. How does this school differ from yours? How is this classroom the same as yours?

_____

_____

2. Why do you think the students are learning about corn and cotton?

_____

_____

❓ Question

3. The Tuskegee Institute operates today as Tuskegee University. Read about this school in books or on safe Internet sites. How has the school changed? How has it remained the same?

_____

_____

4. After studying this photograph, what do you want to know about the students?

_____

_____

💡 Understand

5. Based on this text and the photograph, do you think changing the law was enough to guarantee equal rights for everyone? Explain.

_____

_____

6. Imagine you are the teacher in this 1902 photograph. What difficulties might you encounter at work?

_____

_____

Hit the Road!

At first, cars were just toys. By 1920, Henry Ford had perfected the Model T, often called the Tin Lizzie. This cheap car gave normal Americans the freedom to travel.

The 1930s was the time of the Great Depression. America was hit by drought, which led to hard times. Dust storms killed crops. Starving grasshoppers ate what was left. People in the Dust Bowl states suffered terribly. Many lost their homes. Millions of farmers headed west for work. How did they get to Washington, Oregon, and California? Their sturdy Model T cars.

Photographs documented the lives of these people. Arthur Rothstein photographed this migrant family. He took this photograph in July 1936 near Missoula, Montana. Vernon Evans was from Lemmon, South Dakota. He had packed his family into his car and left home. Evans was hoping to find work in Washington's Yakima Valley. It was hop-picking season there. The trip from Lemmon to Yakima was over 1,000 miles. Evans' Model T could drive 200 miles a day. The family slept in a tent and started off again in the morning.

Library of Congress, LC-USF34-005009-D

Hit the Road!

Originally, cars were just toys. By 1920, Henry Ford's Model T was cheap enough for normal people to buy. It was sometimes called the Tin Lizzie. Americans now had the freedom to drive wherever there were roads.

The 1930s was the decade of the Great Depression. The country was hit by drought, which led to hard times. Dust storms killed crops and starving grasshoppers ate what was left. People in the Dust Bowl states suffered terribly, many losing their homes. Millions of farmers headed west in search of work. How did they get to Washington, Oregon, and California? In their Model T cars.

Photographers documented the struggles of these migrants. Arthur Rothstein took this photograph in July 1936 near Missoula, Montana. Vernon Evans had packed up his family and left his home in Lemmon, South Dakota. It was hop-picking season in Washington's Yakima Valley. Evans was hoping to find work. The journey was more than 1,000 miles. Evan's Model T could cover only 200 miles a day, so the family slept in a tent at night and started off again in the morning.

Library of Congress, LC-USF34-005009-D

Hit the Road!

Originally, cars were merely expensive toys. However, by 1920, Henry Ford's cheap Model T, sometimes called the Tin Lizzie, had given regular Americans the freedom to travel wherever a road went.

In the 1930s, the country was hit by years of drought. Crops that survived fierce dust storms were eaten by flocks of starving grasshoppers. People in the Dust Bowl states lost their farms. Millions of farmers headed for Washington, Oregon, and California, hoping to find work. How did they get there? In their reliable and easy-to-fix Model T cars.

Photographers documented the struggles of migrant farmers during the Great Depression. Arthur Rothstein took this photograph in July 1936 near Missoula, Montana. Vernon Evans had packed up his family and left his home in Lemmon, South Dakota. It was hop-picking season in Washington's Yakima Valley, and Evans was hoping to find work. The journey was more than 1,000 miles. Evan's Model T could cover only 200 miles a day, so the family slept in a tent at night and resumed their journey in the morning.

Library of Congress, LC-USF34-005009-D

Hit the Road!

 Investigate

1. Why do you think the car has stopped? Where do you think these people are going?

_____

_____

2. The subject of the photograph appears in the middle of the photograph. What else do you see? What does that tell you about where this photo was taken?

_____

_____

? Question

3. After studying this photograph, which person do you want to know more about? Why?

_____

_____

4. Looking at this photo, what do you think these migrant workers brought from home? Describe what they would have left behind. Use complete sentences.

_____

_____

Understand

5. Describe how this father might have felt at the time of this photograph.

_____

_____

6. Find out more about the photographs Arthur Rothstein took during the Great Depression. Why do you think he took this photo? Did photographs like this help?

_____

_____

Riding the Rails

The first train chugged down the tracks in 1830. The track was only 13 miles long. But, that was long enough. Americans understood trains could move many people and goods. In 1869, railroad tracks from the West Coast and the East Coast met. This created America's first transcontinental railway.

Settlers had long been moving west. Deserts and mountains were difficult to cross. A trip by stagecoach could take months. It took just 10 days to cross the entire country on a train. More and more people headed west. Trains carried wheat and cotton to factories. They carried flour and clothing to towns.

This sketch appeared in *Frank Leslie's Illustrated Newspaper* on September 24, 1881. President Garfield had been shot. He wanted to return to New Jersey. Doctors insisted that the president travel by train. Rail workers had to work through the night of September 5, 1881. They built a short track from the station to Garfield's cottage. The president died two weeks later. His body was taken, by train, back to Washington.

WORKMEN LAYING THE NEW RAILROAD TRACK ON THE NIGHT OF SEPTEMBER 5TH.

Library of Congress, LC-USZ6-2102

Riding the Rails

The first train lumbered down the tracks in 1830. The railroad was only 13 miles long. But, that distance was enough to prove that trains could move large numbers of people and goods. In 1869, railroad tracks from the West Coast and the East Coast met. This created America's first transcontinental railway.

Settlers had long been moving west, but deserts and mountains were huge obstacles. A trip by stagecoach could take months. With the railroad, it took 10 days to cross the entire country. More and more people headed west. Trains carried wheat and cotton to factories, and flour and clothing to towns.

This sketch appeared in *Frank Leslie's Illustrated Newspaper* on September 24, 1881. President Garfield had been shot and wished to return to New Jersey. Doctors wanted the president to travel by train. Rail workers labored through the night of September 5, 1881, to build a short track, or spur, from the Elberon train station to Garfield's cottage. The president died two weeks later. His body was transported, by rail, back to Washington.

WORKMEN LAYING THE NEW RAILROAD TRACK ON THE NIGHT OF SEPTEMBER 5TH.

Library of Congress, LC-USZ6-2102

Riding the Rails

The first train lumbered down the tracks in 1830. The railroad was only 13 miles long, but that distance was enough to prove trains could transport large numbers of people and goods. In 1869, railroad tracks from the West Coast and East Coast met, linking America's first transcontinental railway.

Settlers had long been migrating west, but deserts and mountains were enormous obstacles. A journey by stagecoach could take months. With the railroad, it took 10 days to cross the entire country. More and more people headed west. Trains carried wheat and cotton to factories, and flour and clothing to towns.

This sketch appeared in *Frank Leslie's Illustrated Newspaper* on September 24, 1881. President Garfield had been shot and was hoping to recuperate in New Jersey. Doctors insisted the president travel by rail. Rail workers toiled through the night of September 5, 1881, to lay a short track, or spur, from the Elberon train station to Garfield's cottage. The president died two weeks later, and his body was transported, by rail, back to Washington.

WORKMEN LAYING THE NEW RAILROAD TRACK ON THE NIGHT OF SEPTEMBER 5TH.

Library of Congress, LC-USZ6-2102

Riding the Rails

 Investigate

1. What did you notice first about the sketch? Why?

   _____

   _____

2. What did you think while examining this sketch? How does knowing what event inspired this sketch change your reaction to it? Explain.

   _____

   _____

? Question

3. Based on the text, why do you think this sketch appeared in the newspaper almost three weeks after the event it shows? Why didn't it appear immediately? Explain.

   _____

   _____

4. Do you think everyone wanted this piece of railroad built? Do you think everyone wanted the transcontinental railroad built? Why or why not?

   _____

   _____

Understand

5. In what ways did the transcontinental railroad change the country? Explain.

   _____

   _____

6. How different do you think life is for railroad workers today? Read about railroad workers in books or on safe Internet sites.

   _____

   _____

The Worker as a Machine

Assembly lines changed the way things are made. Simple assembly lines had been used before 1900. But, carmaker Henry Ford perfected the assembly line for the Ford Motor Company. His first car took 12 hours to make. Ford was sure he could make more cars in less time. He created machines for the small tasks. He studied his workers' movements. He wanted each job to be simple.

By 1914, the same car took just 90 minutes to build. Motors ran conveyor belts and pulleys. These belts moved car parts from place to place. Workers stayed in one spot, doing one job. They didn't work on the whole car. The assembly lines moved past the workers.

This photograph was taken around 1914. It shows assembly-line workers in Crockett, California. The California & Hawaii Sugar Company imported sugar cane from Hawaii. These workers are filling, weighing, and sewing up bags of sugar. One worker could sew up to 17 bags per minute. C & H still exists today. Robots perform many of its assembly-line jobs.

Library of Congress, LC-USZ62-107113

The Worker as a Machine

Assembly lines changed the way things are made. They had been used in British shipbuilding years before 1900. But, carmaker Henry Ford perfected the system for the Ford Motor Company. His first car took 12 hours to make, but Ford was sure he could produce more cars at a lower price. He created machinery for the small tasks and studied his workers. Their movements needed to be as simple as possible.

By 1914, the same car took just 90 minutes to build. Motors ran conveyor belts and pulleys. These belts moved car parts from place to place within the factory. Workers stayed in one spot, doing one job. They didn't work on the whole product.

This photograph was taken around 1914. It shows workers on an assembly line in Crockett, California. The California & Hawaii Sugar Company imported sugar cane from Hawaii. These operatives, or workers, are filling, weighing, and sewing up bags of sugar. One worker could sew up to 17 bags per minute. C & H still exists today, but robots perform many of its assembly-line jobs.

Library of Congress, LC-USZ62-107113

The Worker as a Machine

Assembly lines changed the way things are made. They had been used in British shipbuilding a century before they were used in the United States. Carmaker Henry Ford perfected the system. His first car took 12 hours to assemble, but Ford was convinced he could produce more cars at a lower price. He created machinery for the small tasks and studied his workers' motions. Each movement needed to be as simple as possible.

By 1914, the same car took only 90 minutes to build. Motorized conveyor belts and pulleys transported every piece to the next step in the manufacturing process. Workers stayed in one place, performing a single task instead of working on an entire car.

This photograph, taken around 1914, shows workers on an assembly line in Crockett, California. The California & Hawaii Sugar Company imported sugar cane from Hawaii. These operatives, or workers, are filling, weighing, and sewing up bags of sugar. One worker could sew up to 17 bags per minute. C & H still exists today, but many of its assembly-line jobs are performed by robots.

Library of Congress, LC-USZ62-107113

The Worker as a Machine

 Investigate

I.   What is happening in this photograph?

   _____

   _____

2.   What kinds of simple machines do you see? Explain how you think these machines work.

   _____

   _____

 Question

3.   After studying this photograph, what do you want to learn more about?

   _____

   _____

4.   This photograph shows what the sugar workers could see. Describe the sounds and smells workers might hear and smell. Explain the source of those sounds and smells.

   _____

   _____

 Understand

5.   Imagine working on an assembly line in 1914. Describe what you do. Then, explain how performing your job makes you feel.

   _____

   _____

6.   Based on the text and photograph, do you think assembly lines are a good idea? Explain your answer.

   _____

   _____

A Complex Man

Benjamin Franklin (1706–1790) was always thinking about how things worked. He wanted to make them better.

Franklin was a printer and writer. He published the truth. Poor people couldn't afford to buy books. Franklin created a library so they could borrow books instead.

Franklin was a scientist. He was an inventor too. He flew a kite in a storm to see if lightning was electricity. He took ocean temperatures to learn about currents. He created bifocals so he wouldn't have to keep taking off his glasses.

Franklin signed the Declaration of Independence and the Constitution. He made deals with England and France. During his lifetime, Franklin visited eight countries. Most people traveled only 10 miles from home.

Tompkins Harrison Matteson was an artist. He was called the "Pilgrim Painter." He painted patriotic scenes. Matteson was born after Franklin had died. He studied older paintings of Franklin. This picture was painted around 1846. This was the beginning of the Colonial Revival period. Many Americans wanted to remember their past.

Library of Congress, LC-USZ62-19451

A Complex Man

Benjamin Franklin (1706–1790) was always thinking about how things worked and how to make them better.

Franklin was a printer who published the truth. He wrote with a sense of humor. Franklin knew poor people couldn't afford books, so he created a borrowing library.

Franklin was a scientist and an inventor. He flew a kite in a storm to discover if lightning was electricity. He recorded ocean temperatures to track currents. He created bifocals so he wouldn't have to keep removing his glasses.

Franklin signed the Declaration of Independence and the Constitution. He made treaties with England and France. He visited eight countries at a time when few people moved 10 miles from home.

Tompkins Harrison Matteson was an artist born after Franklin's death. Matteson studied older paintings of Franklin. He was called the "Pilgrim Painter" because of his patriotic paintings. Matteson painted this picture around 1846. This was the beginning of the Colonial Revival period, a time when Americans wanted to remember their past.

Library of Congress, LC-USZ62-19451

A Complex Man

Benjamin Franklin (1706–1790) was always thinking about how things worked and how to make them better.

Franklin was a printer who printed the truth. He wrote with a sense of humor. Franklin knew poor people couldn't afford books, so he created a library where books could be borrowed.

Franklin was a scientist and an inventor. He flew a kite in a storm to discover if lightning was electricity. He recorded ocean temperatures to track currents. He created bifocals so he wouldn't have to keep removing his glasses.

Franklin signed the Declaration of Independence and the Constitution. He negotiated treaties with England and France. He visited eight countries, at a time when people usually traveled only 10 miles from home.

Tompkins Harrison Matteson was an artist born after Franklin's death. Known as the "Pilgrim Painter," Matteson was famous for patriotic scenes. He painted this picture around 1846, after studying older artists' paintings of Franklin. This marked the beginning of the Colonial Revival period, a time when Americans wanted to remember their past.

Library of Congress, LC-USZ62-19451

A Complex Man

Investigate

1. Divide the picture into quarters. Describe what you see in each section of the painting.

   _____

   _____

2. Why do you think Matteson painted Franklin in these surroundings? Explain.

   _____

   _____

Question

3. After studying this painting, what aspect of Franklin's life do you want to learn more about?

   _____

   _____

4. Which of Franklin's accomplishments do not appear in the painting? Look in books and on safe Internet sites to find out.

   _____

   _____

Understand

5. What do you think makes Franklin such an important historical figure? Why?

   _____

   _____

6. Why do you think Matteson chose to paint Benjamin Franklin? How do you think Matteson wanted people to react to this painting?

   _____

   _____

Passenger to Freedom

Harriet Tubman (ca. 1820–1913) was a slave. She grew up on a Maryland plantation. In 1849, her owner died. Knowing she'd be sold and taken from her family, Tubman escaped.

Tubman became a *conductor* on the Underground Railroad. This group helped runaway slaves. Tubman returned to Maryland many times to help family members. The Fugitive Slave Act became law in 1850. This made it unsafe for escaped slaves everywhere. Tubman had to take the slaves to Canada. She made almost 20 trips. Tubman rescued over 200 people, including her parents.

During the Civil War, Tubman was a nurse. She was a spy too. Tubman talked to slaves along South Carolina's coast. These slaves became army scouts. They looked for information. The scouts found groups of slaves that could be freed by the Union army.

Tubman lived in Auburn, New York. She supported African American schools. She worked for women's rights. She even donated her home to needy people. That is where she died.

This photograph of Tubman was taken by Harvey B. Lindsley between 1860 and 1875.

Library of Congress, LC-USZ62-7816

Passenger to Freedom

Harriet Tubman (ca. 1820–1913) grew up as a slave on a Maryland plantation. In 1849, her owner died. Knowing she'd be sold and separated from her family, Tubman escaped.

Tubman became a *conductor* on the Underground Railroad. The Underground Railroad helped runaway slaves. Tubman returned to Maryland many times to help family and friends. The Fugitive Slave Act became law in 1850. This law made it unsafe for escaped slaves, so Tubman had to bring her *passengers* to Canada. She made nearly 20 trips, mostly from Maryland. She rescued over 200 people, including her parents.

During the Civil War, Tubman worked as a nurse and spy. She contacted slaves along the South Carolina coast. These scouts then identified groups of slaves that could be freed by Union forces.

Tubman settled in Auburn, New York. She raised money for African American schools and worked for women's rights. She even donated her home to people in need, where she died at the age of 93.

This photograph of Tubman was taken by Harvey B. Lindsley between 1860 and 1875.

Library of Congress, LC-USZ62-7816

Passenger to Freedom

Harriet Tubman (ca. 1820–1913) grew up as a slave on a Maryland plantation. In 1849, her owner died. Knowing she'd be sold and separated from her family, Tubman escaped.

Tubman became a *conductor* on the Underground Railroad, a group that helped runaway slaves. She returned to Maryland many times to help family and friends. The Fugitive Slave Act of 1850 made it unsafe for escaped slaves, so Tubman had to bring her *passengers* to Canada. She made almost 20 trips, mostly from Maryland, and rescued over 200 people, including her parents.

During the Civil War, Tubman worked as a nurse and spy. She contacted slaves along the South Carolina coast, who then helped identify groups of slaves to be freed by Union forces.

Tubman settled in Auburn, New York. She raised money for African American schools and worked for women's rights. She even donated her home to people in need, where she died at the age of 93.

This photograph of Tubman was taken by Harvey B. Lindsley between 1860 and 1875.

Library of Congress, LC-USZ62-7816

Passenger to Freedom

 Investigate

1. The photographer has staged Tubman with some of her belongings. What are these belongings? Why do you think this was done?

    _____

    _____

2. Looking only at the photo, what kind of person do you think Tubman was? Explain.

    _____

    _____

Question

3. After reading the text, study the photograph again. Do you think the photo accurately shows Tubman's personality and strengths? Why or why not?

    _____

    _____

4. Why do you think Tubman was able to rescue slaves from Maryland so many times without being caught?

    _____

    _____

Understand

5. Imagine being a conductor on the Underground Railroad. What problems might you have encountered? Write your answer in complete sentences.

    _____

    _____

6. What exactly was the Fugitive Slave Act and how did it make Tubman's job more dangerous? Look in books and on safe Internet sites to find out.

    _____

    _____

A Man of Many Words

Words were Frederick Douglass's (ca. 1818–1895) key to freedom. Douglass was born a slave in Maryland. His father was possibly his white master. Douglass was sent to a slave breaker for "training." This brutal year changed his life. At 20, Douglass escaped.

Douglass spoke out against slavery. He was a strong speaker. Some people didn't think he had been a slave. Douglass wrote his first autobiography in 1845. He had to flee to England to escape recapture. British antislavery supporters paid for Douglass's freedom.

Douglass moved to Rochester, New York. He ran an antislavery newspaper. He gave many speeches. Douglass's home was an Underground Railroad station. He believed everyone was equal. He also believed in women's rights.

During the Civil War, Douglass talked black troops into joining the Union army. He moved to Washington, DC. There, he worked for justice until his death.

This photograph was taken between 1850 and 1860. The photograph was printed on paper that had been soaked in a mixture of egg whites, or *albumen*. This type of photograph is called an *albumen* print.

Library of Congress, LC-USZ62-15887

A Man of Many Words

Words were Frederick Douglass's (ca. 1818–1895) key to freedom. Douglass was born a slave in Maryland. His father was possibly his white master. A teenaged Douglass was sent to a slave breaker for "training." This brutal year changed his life. At age 20, Douglass escaped.

Douglass started to speak out against slavery. He was such a powerful speaker that people doubted his story. Douglass wrote his first autobiography in 1845. He had to flee to England to avoid recapture. British abolitionist supporters bought Douglass's freedom.

Douglass moved to Rochester, New York. He ran an abolitionist newspaper and lectured widely. Douglass's home was an Underground Railroad station. He believed in equality for all. He also supported women's rights.

Throughout the Civil War, Douglass persuaded black troops to join the Union army, and promoted civil rights. He moved to Washington, DC, remaining politically active until his death.

This photograph was taken between 1850 and 1860. The photograph was printed on paper that had been soaked in a salty mixture of egg whites, or *albumen*. This type of photograph is called an *albumen* print.

Library of Congress, LC-USZ62-15887

A Man of Many Words

Words were Frederick Douglass's (ca. 1818–1895) key to freedom. Douglass was born a slave in Maryland; his father was possibly his white master. A teenage Douglass was sent to a slave breaker for "training." This brutal year changed his life. Douglass escaped at age 20.

Almost immediately, Douglass spoke out against slavery. His speeches were so intelligent that people doubted his story. Douglass wrote his first autobiography in 1845 and had to flee to England to avoid recapture. British abolitionist supporters purchased Douglass's freedom.

Douglass moved to Rochester, New York, where he published an abolitionist newspaper. He lectured extensively. Douglass was committed to equality, including women's rights. His home was an Underground Railroad station.

Throughout the Civil War, Douglass recruited black troops for the Union army and spoke in support of civil rights. He moved to Washington, DC, remaining politically active until his death.

This albumen print was made between 1850 and 1860. The photo paper had been soaked in a salty solution of egg whites, or *albumen*. The albumen print was the most common form of paper photograph from the 1850s to the 1890s.

Library of Congress, LC-USZ62-15887

A Man of Many Words

Investigate

1. Study the photograph. Describe Frederick Douglass in your own words.

   _____

   _____

2. Do you think Douglass looked like a slave? Why or why not?

   _____

   _____

? Question

3. Why do you think Douglass kept speaking out against slavery even after he was freed?

   _____

   _____

4. Why do you think Douglass moved to the capital?

   _____

   _____

Understand

5. Imagine you are a slave. How would that make you feel? What would that kind of life be like? Explain.

   _____

   _____

6. Some people didn't believe Douglass had been a slave. Why do you think they felt that way?

   _____

   _____

Home Sweet Home

People have always needed homes. Long ago, homes were made of available resources. There were often few available resources.

The Plains Indians followed the buffalo. Their tepees were made of poles and buffalo hides. Tepees could be moved easily. Some settlers had many trees. They needed only an ax to build a log cabin. These homes lasted decades. The southwest desert was hot and dry. Settlers there built adobe homes from dried bricks of mud.

An 1862 law gave settlers free land. People headed west. Few trees grew on the western plains. Those settlers used sod for their new homes. Sod is a piece of ground made of grass and plant roots. Strips of sod were cut from the ground. The strips were stacked, making walls. Sod houses were sometimes built into hillsides so that only the fronts of the houses needed to be covered with sod.

This 1886 photograph was taken by Solomon Butcher. He later created a book celebrating sod houses. The Sylvester Rawding family lived north of Sargent, Custer County, Nebraska. This photograph shows them in front of their sod house.

Library of Congress, LC-USZ62-8276

Home Sweet Home

People have always needed shelter. Long ago, available resources dictated the type of shelter that was built. The available resources were often limited.

The Plains Indians followed the buffalo. Their tepees, made of poles and buffalo hides, were portable. Since trees were scarce, they kept their poles with them. Some settlers had too many trees. The only tool they needed to build a log house was an ax. These cabins lasted decades. In the southwest desert, people needed shelter from heat and wind. Settlers there used bricks of dried mud to build adobe homes.

After the Homestead Act of 1862, settlers flocked west. Few trees grew on the western plains. Many of those settlers built sod houses, or soddies. The walls were made of strips of sod, cut from prairie grass. Soddies were often built into hillsides so that only the fronts of the houses needed to be covered with sod.

This 1886 photograph was taken near Sargent, Custer County, Nebraska, by Solomon Butcher. He later created a book celebrating sod houses. The Sylvester Rawding family is photographed in front of their sod house.

Library of Congress, LC-USZ62-8276

Home Sweet Home

People have always needed shelter. Available natural resources often decided the type of shelter that could be built. The available resources were sometimes` quite limited.

The Plains Indians followed the buffalo. Their tepees, made of poles and buffalo hides, were portable. Since trees were scarce, they carried their poles with them. Some settlers had an abundance of trees. The only tool needed to build a log house was an ax. Their sturdy cabins lasted decades. People in the southwest desert needed shelter from heat and wind. Settlers used bricks of dried mud to construct adobe homes that remained cool in the summer.

After the Homestead Act of 1862, settlers flocked west. The treeless soil was fertile for crops but not suitable for making bricks. Sod houses, or soddies, were made of stacked strips of sod cut from the prairie floor and were frequently built into hillsides so that only the fronts of the houses needed to be covered with sod.

This 1886 photo was taken near Sargent, Custer County, Nebraska, by Solomon Butcher. Butcher later created a book celebrating sod houses. The Sylvester Rawding family is photographed in front of their sod house.

Library of Congress, LC-USZ62-8276

Name _____

Home Sweet Home

 Investigate

1. What did you notice first about the photo? Why?

   _____

   _____

2. Describe the house.

   _____

   _____

 Question

3. Why do you think the animals are part of the photograph?

   _____

   _____

4. Look closely at the children. What do you notice about the boys? What do you notice about the girl?

   _____

   _____

 Understand

5. Imagine living in a sod house in 1886. Describe how your life would be different.

   _____

   _____

6. What kind of food is on the table in the photograph? Look in books and on safe Internet sites to find out what this food represented to the settlers.

   _____

   _____

Gold Fever

There have been many gold rushes. In 1829, gold was found in Georgia. The land belonged to the Cherokee tribe. People came for the gold.

An 1848 gold rush sent 250,000 prospectors to California. They hoped to get rich. By 1850, California's population was so high it became a state. San Francisco and Sacramento grew into big cities. Some people did get rich. But, most didn't make enough money to even return home. In 1859, gold was found at Pike's Peak. The city of Denver, Colorado, grew too.

Gold was discovered in the Black Hills in 1874. These hills were in Dakota Territory where the Sioux Indians lived. More people came for gold. In 1897, miners headed to Alaska. Even the cold could not stop them in their search for gold.

This 1889 photograph was taken by John C. H. Grabill. Three gold prospectors are panning for gold in Rockerville, South Dakota. Spriggs, Lamb, and Dillon fill pans with sand. Then, they swirl the pans in water. Heavy gold pieces sink. Fine gold powder sticks to the edges.

Library of Congress, LC-USZ62-7120

Gold Fever

Gold rushes are not uncommon. In 1829, gold was found on land belonging to the Cherokee tribe. Eager miners flooded northern Georgia. The small tourist town of Dahlonega (Cherokee for "yellow money") still exists today.

An 1848 gold rush sent 250,000 people west, hoping to strike it rich. By 1850, California's population was so high it became a state. Some miners did get rich, but most didn't make enough money to even return home. San Francisco and Sacramento grew out of this gold rush. In 1859, when gold was found at Colorado's Pike's Peak, it was Denver's turn to grow.

In 1874, gold was found in the Dakota's Black Hills. People swarmed into Sioux Indian territory for gold. In 1897, miners headed north. Even the Alaskan cold did not stop their gold fever.

This 1889 photograph was taken by John C. H. Grabill. Three prospectors are panning for gold in Rockerville, South Dakota. Spriggs, Lamb, and Dillon fill pans with sand and swirl them in water. Heavy gold pieces sink. Fine gold powder sticks to the edges.

2357. "We have It Rich." Washing and panning gold, Rockerville, Dak. Old timers, Spriggs, Lamb and Dillon at work. Photo and copyright by Grabill, 1889.

Gold Fever

Gold rushes are not uncommon. In 1829, gold was discovered on land belonging to the Cherokee tribe. Eager prospectors flooded northern Georgia. The small tourist town of Dahlonega (Cherokee for "yellow money") still exists today.

An 1848 gold rush sent 250,000 people west, hoping to strike it rich. By 1850, California's population was so high it became an official state. Some miners did become wealthy, but most didn't make enough money to even return home. San Francisco and Sacramento grew out of this gold rush. A decade later, when gold was found at Colorado's Pike's Peak, it was Denver's turn to flourish.

In 1874, gold in South Dakota's Black Hills sent prospectors swarming into Sioux Indian territory. In 1897, prospectors headed north, braving the bitter Alaskan cold in search of gold.

This 1889 photograph was taken by John C. H. Grabill of Rockerville, South Dakota. Three prospectors, Spriggs, Lamb, and Dillon, are panning for gold. They fill a pan with sand and swirl it in water. Heavy gold pieces sink; fine gold powder sticks to the edges.

Library of Congress, LC-USZ62-7120

Gold Fever

 Investigate

1. What is happening in this photograph? Describe the four subjects in this photograph.

   _____

   _____

2. Describe how the men are dressed. Why are they dressed that way?

   _____

   _____

? Question

3. After studying this photograph, what do you think the water is being used for? If you don't know, look in a book or on safe Internet sites to find out.

   _____

   _____

4. These men are "panning" for gold. In what other ways do people mine for gold?

   _____

   _____

Understand

5. What dangers do these men face? Explain.

   _____

   _____

6. Why would people travel so far in search of gold? Use complete sentences.

   _____

   _____

Beneath the Ice

Seafood, including fish, has been part of our diet since humans started using tools. Fishermen use traps, nets, poles, spears, and even their hands! Winter doesn't stop anglers. Lakes and rivers freeze. But, fish are still active. As long as you can chop a hole in the ice, you can fish.

Ice fishing is different from summer fishing. Summertime anglers need long rods. They cast their lines out into open water. They use reels to wind the lines back. Wintertime anglers fish through small holes. Their rods, called jiggle sticks, are short. The angler jigs the rod up and down. This attracts the fish. When a fish bites the hook, the angler pulls the line out of the ice.

Ice fishing is popular in the northern states. Today, many anglers fish from inside cozy ice shacks. In winter, some frozen lakes look like small villages.

This photograph of a man ice fishing was taken between 1910 and 1915. It was published by the Bain News Service, which was one of the first US news picture agencies.

Library of Congress, LC-DIG-ggbain-10041

Beneath the Ice

Seafood, including fish, has been part of our diet since humans started using tools. Fishermen use traps, nets, poles, spears, and even their hands! Winter doesn't stop anglers. Lakes and rivers freeze, but fish are still active. As long as you're able to chop a hole in the ice, you can fish.

Ice fishing differs from warm-weather fishing. Summertime anglers need long rods to cast their lines out into open water. They use reels to wind the lines back. Wintertime anglers fish through small holes. Their rods, called jiggle sticks, are short. The angler jigs the rod up and down to attract the fish. When a fish bites the hook, the angler pulls the line up out of the ice.

Ice fishing is popular in the northern states. Today, so many anglers fish from inside cozy ice shacks that some frozen lakes look like small villages!

This photograph of a man ice fishing was taken between 1910 and 1915. It was published by the Bain News Service, which was one of the first US news picture agencies.

Library of Congress, LC-DIG-ggbain-10041

Beneath the Ice

Seafood, including fish, has been part of our diet since humans discovered tools. Fishermen use a variety of methods: traps, nets, poles, spears, and even their hands! Hardy anglers don't let winter stop them. Lakes and rivers freeze, but fish are still active! As long as you're able to chop a hole in the ice, you can fish.

Ice fishing differs from warm-weather fishing. Summertime anglers need long rods to cast their lines out into open water, using reels to wind the lines back. Wintertime anglers fish through small holes. They jig their short rods, called jiggle sticks, up and down to attract the fish. When a fish bites the hook, the angler pulls the line up out of the ice.

Ice fishing is popular in the northern states. Today, so many anglers fish from inside cozy ice shacks that some lakes look like small villages!

This photograph of a man ice fishing was taken between 1910 and 1915. It was published by the Bain News Service, one of the first US news picture agencies.

Library of Congress, LC-DIG-ggbain-10041

Name _____

Beneath the Ice

 Investigate

1. Describe the tools shown in this photograph.

   _____

   _____

2. What might have been different about ice fishing then from today?

   _____

   _____

? Question

3. What do you wonder about this man?

   _____

   _____

4. In what other ways do you think this lake was important to this man?

   _____

   _____

Understand

5. Describe the steps you would take to make your own jiggle stick.

   _____

   _____

6. Look at the food in your kitchen. Which foods would you have had a century ago? How would you have gotten them?

   _____

   _____

Answer Key

Page 7
1. Answers will vary. 2. Word clues are *cash*, *dispose*, *highest price*, and *sell*. 3. Answers should be based on research. 4. Mr. Griggs would have paid more for young, strong men than for children, women, or old slaves. He would have paid the most for young, strong, healthy men. 5–6. Answers will vary.

Page 11
1–2. Answers will vary but should be based on the photo. 3. Answers will vary but should be based on research. 4. Answers will vary. 5. Answers will vary but should include reasons. 6. Answers will vary but should be insightful.

Page 15
1. African American men are voting. 2. Answers will vary but may include farmer, businessman, or soldier. 3. The man on the left is white and the men on the right are African American. The African American men's clothing varies, but they are more formally dressed. 4. Answers will vary but may include the subject was under national discussion. 5–6. Answers will vary.

Page 19
1. Answers will vary but may include the shawl, book, dress shoes, hat, or that the boy is clean. 2. Answers will vary. 3. Answers will vary but may include immigrants want to keep their language and culture, which is easier to do when living with similar people. 4. Immigrants must apply for a green card. There are some restrictions. 5–6. Answers will vary.

Page 23
1. Answers will vary but should be based on the photo. 2. basket, rolling pin, pan, bucket; 3. Answers will vary. 4. Answers will vary but should include thoughtful reasoning. 5. Answers will vary but should be insightful. 6. Answers will vary but should be based on research.

Page 27
1. Answers will vary but should be based on the photo. 2. Answers may include they are learning about practical subjects so they can make a living. 3. Answers will vary but should be based on research. 4. Answers will vary. 5. Answers will vary but should include thoughtful reasoning. 6. Answers will vary.

Page 31
1. Answers will vary. 2. power line, fence, hills, grass, path; Answers will vary. 3. Answers will vary. 4. Answers will vary but should include some understanding of the hardship of the times. 5. Answers will vary but should be insightful. 6. Answers should be based on research.

Page 35
1–2. Answers will vary but should be based on the sketch. 3. Answers will vary. 4. Most people wanted to do what it took to save the president's life. Answers will vary but may include that the transcontinental railroad would make life much easier for many people. 5. Answers will vary but may include it made it possible to move goods and people across the country more quickly. 6. Answers will vary but should be based on research.

Page 39
1. Workers are filling, weighing, and sewing sugar bags on assembly line. 2. Answers will vary but may include pulley, inclined plane, or wheel and axle. 3. Answers will vary. 4. Answers will vary but may include grease, dust, sugar, fumes, clanging, or ripping. 5. Answers will vary. 6. Answers will vary but should include thoughtful reasoning.

Page 43
1. Answers may include Franklin, books, a hat, a storm, a lighthouse, glasses, papers, a globe, a scroll, a pen, or a compass. 2. Matteson wanted to show Franklin's accomplishments. 3. Answers will vary. 4. Answers will vary but may include false teeth, a furnace stove, the first fire company, an odometer, etc. 5–6. Answers will vary.

Page 47
1. hat, coat, bible; to show that she liked to dress well, was a lady; 2. Answers will vary. 3. Answers will vary but should be based on the photo and text. 4. Answers will vary but may include that Tubman was African American, solitary, secretive, knew the area, and knew many people. 5. Answers will vary but may include being fined, hurt, or killed if caught. 6. Answers should be based on research.

Page 51
1. Answers will vary but should be based on the photo. 2. Answers will vary but should be based on the photo and include thoughtful reasoning. 3. Answers will vary but should include thoughtful reasoning. 4. Answers will vary but may include that Douglass wanted to help in the work of reconstruction. 5–6. Answers will vary.

Page 55
1. Answers will vary. 2. Answers will vary but may include it is covered with strips of sod, grass is growing on the roof, it has windows and doors, etc. 3. Answers will vary but could include that they were an important part of this family's life. 4. The girl is seated and has clean feet and short hair; the boys are standing and have dirty feet. 5. Answers will vary but should be insightful. 6. Answers will vary but may include that watermelon was a treat and showed the bounty of the land..

Page 59
1. The men are panning for gold and the dog is watching. 2. Answers will vary but could include they are wearing jeans, shirts, boots, and hats. They look shabby, likely because this was a hard way to live. 3. Answers will vary but may include separating dirt from gold. 4. Answers will vary but may include digging for gold. 5. Answers will vary but may include cold, heat, wild animals, starvation, cave-ins, or drowning. 6. Answers will vary but should be insightful.

Page 63
1. Answers will vary but may include a piece of wood, fishing line, pail, basket, or net. 2. Answers will vary but may include fishing alone, eating catch, getting cold, or using just one hole. 3. Answers will vary. 4. Answers will vary but may include drinking, cooking, washing, transportation, or irrigation. 5. Answers will vary but should include using wood or fishing line. 6. Answers will vary but should include thoughtful reasoning.